THE
Little Quirks
THAT
MELT
My Heart

A PARADE OF BEAUTIFUL SOULS: AUTISTIC CHILDREN, AND WHAT THEY GIVE US

Ingrid Jeannis-Desire

Xulon Press
2301 Lucien Way #415
Maitland, FL 32751
407.339.4217
www.xulonpress.com

Paperback ISBN-13: 978-1-66286-671-5
Hard Cover ISBN-13: 978-1-66286-672-2
Ebook ISBN-13: 978-1-66286-673-9

We Love Because He First Loved Us
(1 John 4:19).

Dedication

This book is dedicated particularly to the autistic children I worked with for nearly fifteen years, as well as the autistic population worldwide.

I would like to thank all the parents whose children brought so much joy into my life and those who bring so much joy unto others worldwide.

This is the type of joy that is so genuine and can't be bought but can only be cherished.

This book was inspired as a result of the many years I spent with those children and how much I missed them.

They filled my life with so much joy and for that, I am forever grateful.

These children brought things into my life that will stay always, and my heart is gladdened that I was privileged enough to know each and every one of them.

Table of Contents

Introduction

Each person with autism has a set of strengths and challenges that makes him or her distinctively unique and special.

They express themselves the only way they know how for that is the way that is best for them. With that in mind, it is important that we learn about each unique individual and their distinct ways.

When a child expresses himself or herself, it is his or her way of telling the world, "This is who I am! This is me!" And we should respect, always, the way he or she chooses to do it.

We do them an injustice, and we do ourselves an injustice, when we do not make the effort to know them fully, and when we fail to appreciate the precious moments they give to us.

Each autistic child has communicative characteristics unique to them alone, and that is what makes interacting with them so enlivening and rewarding.

They are truly innocent–in their expressions to us, in their ways of connecting with others, and in their manner of forming relationships. It is not always easy for them, or for us, but the challenges and heart-aches just make the special times more special.

I spent almost fifteen wonderful years with the autistic population, and I wouldn't change this beau-tiful experience for anything.

When I first started in the field, I didn't expect to be in awe and feel so rich and empowered. This was nothing short of amazing!

Don't get me wrong, I'm not saying things were peachy and rosy all the time.

Working with autistic children is a real challenge, but at the same time, it was very fulfilling. I grew as a person, and most certainly as a professional, because of these children.

An opportunity to be a part of their world was an opportunity to learn how to forge ties with those who cannot communicate in an ordinary manner, but who need love and support just as much as the rest of us.

Over the course of those years, I fell in love with my students and with all of the idiosyncrasies that made each of them unique and special in their own way.

I looked forward to going to work each day to spend time with them and to interact with them, learning–as much as I could learn–to see the world through their eyes.

Sometimes learning could mean just being next to them and taking part in their activities, for many of them did not speak or they did not know how to interact in a social setting. I also believe that, in some instances, it was possible that some were not even aware of my presence. But my being near them, as a silent supporter and protector, was as important to me as it was to them.

And it was equally important to me that, as much as it was possible, I got to know the person. There was a real person residing within each of my students, and I wanted to get to know that person – for their sake, and for my own. I wanted to know them even if getting to know them was very hard, even if that young person was unable to speak or interact, and even if they were **unaware of the people surrounding them.**

With some of them, it took time to establish rapport, but with others, it took merely weeks, even days.

All in all, I got to know them, and in the process, I earned the badge of friendship. *They began looking forward to interacting with me,* whatever that meant to them, which is how these relationships build into something that you carry around in your heart for the rest of your life; the little quirks that melt my heart.

Dear readers, don't underestimate the autistic population.

They possess strengths, skills, and traits that no one else has. They own their unique set of abilities and excel at them,

Regardless of how severe their disabilities are.

There is always a way to communicate what one wants to express. These children found a way. Autistic children often communicate with a purpose to receive something, to have their needs met. It is at these times when they are most expressive.

These expressions may not be how we would express ourselves, but it is the best way they know how to convey their needs.

I learned their nuances of communication. It took me time to learn some of them while others I picked up quite quickly.

The best part of it was when I realized these antics or idiosyncratic expressions were intended for me only.

I was amazed how they were able to use non-verbal gestures to express what they wanted, and from whom they wanted it.

At times, some of these loving rituals would only unveil themselves in a certain environment; when those moments occurred when I was present, they warmed my heart.

I am sharing these beautiful sentiments and nuances with you because that's all I have left of the population I worked with for many years.

As a school, we went through many challenges which were not always easy to tackle, but we did it. It was not always a honeymoon period.

But our eyes were always on the prize: our children, our angels.

The goals were, without a doubt, to meet all of their needs despite how insurmountable the obstacles were on many occasions.

But we recognized our duties to them, and to ourselves, and we always worked to give them the best possible support and love. Always, we sought to ensure that they were okay and not suffering from the many challenges that accompany being autistic.

They were darlings, interesting and different, fun to be with and, at times, very comical and not even aware of the joy they brought. They were blessings to us, and they did as all children do: they tried to have fun; they embraced life as much as they could. *And they even cracked jokes in their own special, unique, ways.*

When I first arrived at my former school, the place where I would devote myself for 15 challenging but wonderful years, I knew very little about the autistic population.

I was excited to learn about them so I could be productive and able to contribute not only on an administrative level, but a personal level with the children.

Every day, I looked forward to coming to work, not only to ensure the daily successful operation of the school, but to spend time with the students and get to know them.

Each day was a new day, a new beginning. Each moment was new, not knowing what to anticipate next as things were developing and changing at any given moment.

It was a lot to take in, and not knowing what was causing the constant changes did not help, but I was determined and patient and, at the end, it paid off.

Not to mention that having these children be themselves was one of the things that kept me going even in the most trying times.

I remembered them because they warmed my heart in times of despair, weariness, and lack of motivation.

In the pages to follow, I wish to share precious stories about some of the incredible children with whom I was blessed to work.

I've also given a great deal of thought to the formatting of this book. Each and every story has special meaning to me, but I didn't want this to be just another book, because it's not just another book.

This is a book about special people and special memories. And so, with that in mind, this book is not arranged chronologically, but arranged according to special memories involving special people. I hope that, by doing it this way, I can impress upon everyone how unique our autistic community, whether child or adult, is, and how much their presence invigorates the lives around them, especially my very own.

And I'd like to think that I gave something back to them, as well.

And for that, I am forever grateful.

The Pacer

One of the most memorable students I encountered during my career was a young man I came across during my second day of work in the midst of an otherwise uneventful circuit of the classrooms.

Brief introduction: This young man was seemingly always by himself, evidently did not engage with others, and it seemed never showed interest in anything or anyone. He hardly attended to any task and liked being by himself. There was, we would come to learn, a vigorous mind behind the veil, but it would take some doing before we would be allowed to see it.

Since I had just started at the school, I was so excited to visit the classes. As I was about to step into the classroom, a student ran out the door, clearly upset, and hit the first person he saw… me.

After that day, I took a special interest in his activities and personality. I noticed that he could not sit still for long and would always get up from his chair and start pacing.

Each time I visited his classroom after that day, I would take the time to stop by his desk for a second to check on him and attempt to make conversation.

I then decided to start walking alongside him whenever he paced back and forth.

It took a while to develop a relationship with him. Within a few months, he began to trust me. He was placed in a different classroom. I did not waiver, I continued my pattern and was consistent. I should add as well that I followed protocol and was in alignment with his behavior plan as was the classroom staff.

After some times of following him around and talking to him, though he was nonverbal and intellectually very challenged,

I won him over due to the attention I gave him. I can only guess he began to expect to see me in the classroom and looked forward to those moments.

Then one day, as I was following him around, he stopped and looked back at me twice. I couldn't help but smile inwardly. Finally, we were building rapport!

On another day as I continued to converse with him and follow him around, even though the dialogue was always one-way and because he never gave any inclination that he understood.

To my surprise, he turned and took my hand as he was walking fast paced. He kept looking back at me since I couldn't seem to catch up with him.

He made my day that day!

The quirks that melt my heart began!

From that day on, each time I visited the class, he would come and grab my hand before I even approached him, and we would walk back and forth in the classroom.

I would then tell him "thank you" and go on my way.

Since the teacher discovered that we became friends, he would use my visit as an incentive to encourage the student to sit still for a minute to complete a short task or two.

I was much obliged!

Fortunately, this approach did encourage him to accomplish some tasks.

Those beautiful quirks extended outside of the classroom, related services, special subjects, and the cafeteria.

Every time he saw me, he would veer away from his class and come to me. I, in turn, would engage him in some activities and then go on my way to visit other classes.

During another visit, he decided that he would not let me go. I had to explain to him that I had a meeting and would come for another visit the next day.

He listened, then looked at me and let me go. I could tell he understood the gist of what I was saying.

However, he would only let go of me when I addressed him and not when other people told him to let go.

This became our routine. If anyone attempted to remove his hand while he was holding onto me, he would become aggressive toward them, so they would not interfere.

I finally realized that if I had to be at a meeting, I couldn't visit his class as he would not let me go easily.

Interestingly, after school, I would see him in passing at his residence since he was in a twenty-four-hour residential-school program within the same building.

He would come to me and stand at my side. I would then walk him back to his group while signaling the staff not to intervene so as to not cause a ruckus.

The more time I spent with him, the more I discovered that he was a smart young man. I realized this when I visited his class during lunch in the cafeteria as I did every day for all of the classes.

One particular day, he decided to take me on a walk to get coffee in another room as it was his favorite treat.

As I walked with him, the staff walked behind us and went on to prepare the coffee, and then I walked him back to his seat in the home economic room where he was having lunch.

Once he got there, he took the coffee, poured it in the sink, took my hand again, and walked me back to the coffee room.

There he handed me a cup to prepare the coffee for him. The teacher, teacher aide, and I had a good laugh. We said, "He is smart!"

We became buddies. He melted my heart and happy memories of him put a smile on my face every time I think about his lovable and inimitable ways.

There was only the one of him.

After he graduated, I thought that he would forget about me, but that was not the case. He was still living in the same residence while waiting for an adult placement, and thus, whenever I would bump into him after school coming from his day habilitation, he would still come to me.

I realized then that I had made myself a friend for life.

Our children don't ask for much—

Just someone to genuinely care for them and guide them.

They know when they are loved – and they depend upon the love we give them to help them find a foundation as they grapple with the world around them.

Silent Strength

This next angel was also non-verbal, very intel-lectually challenged, and just too cute for words. But, like my other angels, she, too, found a way to com-municate her warmth and love.

Brief introduction: Her life was not an easy one. She had many complications. My angel was frail and required extensive care and very close supervision 24 hours a day. She was noninteractive and needed assistance with basically all her needs. She was quiet and not aware of much of what was happening around her.

Her coordination and gait were always weak and unsteady, and she was always very delicate. At times, I would attempt to hold on to her hands to assist her with tracing or picking up a puzzle piece.

It was hard for her.

I would sit next to her and speak to her whenever I visited her classroom.

She would be totally non-involved and non-interactive, appearing as if she was not paying attention or processing what I was saying.

I was not aware that she understood what was happening around her. So, **imagine my surprise when she suddenly showed her sassy personality!**

I was utterly astonished!

She was able to single me out one day.

Every time I would visit the classroom thereafter, she would automatically stand up and attempt to walk toward me, all the while giggling.

She couldn't open her hand, but she would use her body or arm to direct me to where she wanted to go, and since she wasn't able to open the door, she would just stand in front of it, waiting for me to open it.

We would take a walk in the hallway, and she would giggle. During our walk, I would speak to her, pointing at the classwork that was displayed on the wall.

I would touch her work, and she would just continue to giggle the entire time.

When I returned with her to the classroom, she would remain standing until I left.

She wasn't sure if I was still there to take her for another walk, so I would leave the classroom to avoid creating any confusion.

She shocked me one day as I was opening the door to take her to gym class, she used her arm and body to close the door.

I was amazed because I didn't know she had that kind of strength. It was the physical strength borne out of a greater, more vital, inner resolve.

I was stunned in a good way, and I learned a little bit more about her that day:

She was a survivor and knew what she wanted.

We sometimes don't look deep enough past the surface. I always saw her as this fragile, frail young girl who needed protection and to be handled with care, but she fooled and delighted me.

Yes, it's true that she was indeed fragile, but I was notably impressed and proud to see that she had within her the resolve to do things that were hard for her. And I was thrilled beyond words to also see that she had a vibrant personality. There was a steely resolve, and that's what carried her through the most trying times.

Until she graduated, she would always use whatever part of her body she could to let me know where she wanted to go. Her teacher told me that she only did this ritual with me and would only get up to take a walk with me.

The longer I stayed in the classroom, the more she thought I was there to take her for a walk.

She would sit down and then get up to squirm her way to me. I loved those moments.

It made everything worthwhile.

Thumbs Up

I inherited another wonderful student while I was teaching and reinforcing appropriate social behavior. He used to place his hands inside his pants at any given moment; it didn't matter where he was, or who was present.

Brief introduction: This young man was very particular and liked to do things in a unique manner; because of this, getting him to change certain behaviors was not easy. Though each plan was customized to meet each child's needs, it was not easy to get Thumbs Up to follow instructions.

Whenever I would observe this kind of behavior, I would prompt him to remove his hands and then wash them. And if I was afar, I would use a head gesture to indicate it's not appropriate and would guide him to remove his hands and wash.

The behavior was being reinforced within the classroom, but I did my part to reinforce what was being taught when I was in his presence.

Finally, he came to understand that the corrective action was intended to help him when interacting with others, and the behavior was corrected.

However, that was not the end of it.

Specifically, every time he saw me, he would pretend to put his hands in his pants and then use his head to gesture "no" and give me a thumbs up, touching my thumb with his.

This became his little ritual, little quirk, one he shared just with me. The teacher said, "I don't understand—he only does that with you."

Whenever he saw me, he would do this little ritual everywhere without fail—in the classroom, cafeteria, gym, music room, anywhere really.

That was our little interaction. I would ask him how he was doing, and he would whisper "fine" as he did not speak much. Then he would proceed to engage in the ritual.

That was our relationship for years, and I welcomed it every time.

After graduation, I would see him sometimes in the hallway after school as he was coming from day habilitation to his residence.

He would whisper "hi" and pretend to put his hands down his pants and then give me the thumbs up from afar.

It warmed my heart.

Children never forget things or rituals that bring comfort, predictability, love, or nurturing. That is their way of saying,

"I acknowledge you," "I know you," and "I appreciate you."

The Questioner

Another smart young lady kept me on my toes every time I visited.

Brief introduction: This young lady had a lot going on but when she was calm or in a good place, she loved to ask questions but in her own terms and you'd better be ready to answer.

Our relationship was either that she would ignore me when I approached her, or she would approach me with tons of back-to-back questions for which she expected a reply.

For the times she did ignore me, I would speak to her and she would either not reply or would say something impolite. But I never took it personally, because their behaviors were never about us.

I would just go on my way and realize that it was not her day and that I needed to give her space.

There were some occasions when classroom staff told me not to approach her because it was not safe, and at other times, I could see by her facial expression that she was not having a good day.

I would, however, hear stories that she referred to a beautiful black doll as "Ingrid." It made me smile and gave me hope that nothing was lost after all; she was paying attention.

My wish was for all of these children to know that they were special to me even though I was not the one working in the classroom with them attending to their daily needs.

Somehow, I wanted all of them to feel and know that they were special.

When she would ask me a lot of questions pertaining to my life, I would have to answer and be quick about it.

She would also have a serious tone when she was being curious. Then she would press on my shoulder.

Nevertheless, that was her way of connecting with me, and I appreciated it.

Every bridge quietly built, every gentle touch from each of my beloved students, was meant for me. It was their way of telling me that, somewhere in their hearts, I held a special place.

And they certainly held a special place in my heart.

They still do.

The Sunshine Smiler

When I first came for an interview for the position of assistant principal, I was given a tour of one of the classrooms. There was a young man who took a liking to me as soon as I entered the room.

Brief introduction: This young man was a sunshine, a breadth of fresh air, always smiling and very active. On a few occasions, he took me for a walk in the hallway and as much as I wanted to accompany him, I could not keep up. He was too fast.

Though he was nonverbal, he made me feel most welcome by giving me the most beautiful, genuine smile I had ever seen.

He held on to my hands with a bright, shining smile and didn't let go until the tour was over. His teacher shared with me that day that he was a social butterfly. He reached out, with that wonderful smile, and sought connections with the people who inhabited his world.

He decided that I would be his friend from that moment onward.

When I met him he was only 14 years old; he would graduate at 21. And, in all those years, his interaction with me was always constant.

I would visit the classroom every day and he would welcome me in the same manner. He would quickly rush to the door to give me a wide smile and would hold on to my hand and not let go.

If and when another student was attempting to get my attention, he would pull my hands or turn my face toward him.

I would need to bargain with him and try to explain that I'd like to say hello to his classmates.

He would then walk with me and continue to smile.

Furthermore, whenever I would see him, whether it was in or out of the classroom, in the cafeteria, in the library, or in the gym, he would always rush to greet me with a wide, contagious smile and hold on to my hands.

This interaction never wavered, not in all the years we were together.

After his graduation, I missed that genuine, beautiful smile each time I entered his former classroom.

That was his way of telling me that I was special to him and he to me. These children don't ask much of us—only a warm face, a loving heart, and a nurturing hand.

I saw him several years after, in his adult home, and he remembered me and came to me with that big smile and held on to my hand.

They are such precious human beings; they give wholeheartedly and innocently, these children of God.

They will forever be remembered.

The Charmer

The next young man I wish to talk about was a charmer. Though he was non-verbal, he always let me know his needs. He took control.

Brief introduction: This young man at the beginning was withdrawn and would not interact with anyone. I would make it a priority to sit by him and chat with him or took an interest in what he was, or was not, doing weekly.

I developed a special friendship with The Charmer somewhere along the way. I am not even sure, precisely, when and how it started. But he became as curious in me as I was in him. Whenever I visited the classroom, he began to look forward to having me sit by him. He would be flicking the top of his desk with one hand while pulling a chair next to him and gesturing for me to sit down with the other.

Once I sat, he was happy and gave me a sheepish smile and continued to flick. I would chat with him and he would flick and gave me a smile. When he

*was ready to let me leave, he would pull the chair
back and that would be my cue to go.*

He would always look at me with a timid smile when
he saw me and would take hold of my hand or arm.

There was one day when his class was walking in
the hallway to gym class.

He spotted me and automatically approached me,
locking arms with me so we could walk together.

Once he got there, he stopped for water at the
water fountain while our arms were still locked. He
finally let go of my arm before he entered the gym
and gave me that typical sheepish smile.

These routines and patterns of practices were
repeated on many, many occasions, and I was okay
with them, as well.

For I knew that was his way of interacting with me
and letting me know that "I know you, and I appreciate you taking a liking to me."

These children are smart and witty. Let no one
ever forget that! These quirky moments of intimate

bonding led me to appreciate these children even more. They must never be seen as merely statistics.

It is true that they may be intellectually challenged and face many obstacles, including using spoken language itself, but their kind hearts are open to all who want to care for them and guide them.

Several years after graduation, I saw him at a Christmas party held by his group home, and he demonstrated the same warm-hearted rituals that first drew me to him.

He saw me before I saw him, and he pulled out the chair that was for one of his friends and gestured for me to sit down. I greeted him and said, "You remember me!"

It warmed my heart and I teared up inside.

He then gave me that sheepish smile of his and continued to flick his fingers on the table.

We parted after a few minutes as I had come to visit with everyone there.

It pleased and surprised me that these special and invigorating rituals were only done with me.

We can find joy and commonality within one another.

They thrive on the same basic things we all do, which is genuine affection, some attention, and guidance.

They know when someone is being real and wants the best for them.

I believe my relationships with them have always been genuine, nurturing, and simple with no demands, and the consistency of my affection toward them was felt somehow.

Well, at least that is what I told myself.

In essence, rapport building with these children is crucial in order to properly care for, and to attend to, their needs–and to be part of their idiosyncratic world wherein the two greatest characteristics of all are their capacity for love, and their willingness to share their lives with those worthy of it.

They respond to structure, consistency, steadiness, predictability, and good nurturing.

Having them take a liking to me and share some of their unique rituals and expressions of love and affection was a most precious privilege. It is a feeling of gratitude I will carry with me for the rest of my life.

Once you have earned their trust, it is an eternal binding friendship that they will never forget.

And you won't forget it either.

Personally, I found learning their different nuances was an honor.

While they lasted, it made my journey all the more fulfilling.

The Friend Who Made My Day

This young lady could speak, but when asked to, she would not. she had nice handwriting and was among the very few who were aware of when dangers were present and would be quick to steer away from them in a flash.

Brief introduction: This young lady was quiet yet very observant. She had many skills but would not show it unless she was prompted which is typical for some of our students. It was not easy for her to develop relationship so when she finally took an interest I was joyful.

She was a smart young lady. She could copy information from the board accurately and quickly. The teacher would ask her to read the morning news she would oblige but with some hesitation.

When I visited her classroom, I would greet every student before spending some extra time getting to know her.

I was always patient. I didn't ask much and just stayed by her side and complimented her work, hoping to get a precious word or two out of her.

That was all that it took for, lo and behold, she finally spoke to me! From that moment on, a new, lasting friendship was formed.

After I complimented her handwriting, she said clearly, "Thank you," and looked at me. I was shocked!

I proceeded to ask her to read a sentence, and to my bewilderment, she did!

I gave her a high five, and she smiled.

Each time I visited the classroom, she looked up to see me coming to her, and we would chat and exchange words.

At times, during our visit, she would point for me to read, and I would ask her to read in return.

To my astonishment, she called out my name one day as I was entering the classroom and said, "Come, Ingrid!"

I happily went over to her and thanked her for acknowledging my presence, and she smiled.

And so, it became a routine. I would visit, and she would share her work with me and articulate some words.

If she was not having a good day and I happened to be there, she would seek comfort from me or ask me to sit with her and that would help her calm down. She needed those moments to decompress every now and then. Various types of therapeutic interventions were needed for most of our children often times.

It is not easy for the autistic population to seek comfort from anyone when they are not in a good place unless they have come to trust the people who care for them.

I felt humbled that she found some comfort within my presence.

Having her reach out to me in her time of vulnerability spoke volumes to how she regarded me, and knowing my role as the school principal would offer little assistance to her behavioral needs. I was touched.

It was times like these that reminded me of the importance of my work and that I was making a difference one small step at a time.

It was a wonderful feeling that the children found something in my company to be soothing, safe, comforting, and a sense of calmness.

They relied on all of us in the school to help them understand their world, navigate their environment, and know what to expect next.

If I have taken part in providing some of this help to them, then I am blessed.

The Gentle Giant

At the beginning, this young man would not pay me any mind. I would go to him and say hello. He would ignore me, get up, and just start walking around the classroom.

Brief introduction: I love getting to know the students especially when they can't express themselves and or fend for themselves. This young man was tall and huge and behavior can be unpredictable. However, he was the sweetest. He made for a rather hulking image on the outside, but he was soft and gentle on the inside once you got to know him and build a relationship with him.

He was also not one to attend to task. He would do whatever he can to avoid doing class work.

The visits continued in that manner for a while, until one day, I approached him, and he turned and put his face close to mine and smiled.

He then got up, took my hand, and got the bathroom pass hanging on the wall for me to lead him to the bathroom.

I was astounded!

A staff member followed as they would be the ones to care for his bathroom needs. I walked in the hallway with him side by side.

After that, I had earned a new friend. Every time I visited the classroom, he would bring his face to mine, stare in my eyes, then get up and walk.

<u>Those cherished moments are what they are: precious moments that last a lifetime, and that make our chosen careers worth every setback.</u>

Each time he passed by me, he would come to a halt, bring his face to mine with his wide eyes, and laugh, then he would continue to walk. What joy!

At times, I was a bit intimidated as he was very tall and unpredictable, though a sweet giant. That was our connection, our quirk to one another, and I treasured it. Our relationship was of that sort.

The exhibitions of affection and love that characterized my Gentle Giant, which certainly might have seemed odd and which might even have been perceived as unsafe at times, were expressed unconditionally; they were consistent with a loving and innocent mind, and filled with pure love. **These moments I will forever hold dear.**

Don't ever think these children are not paying attention because they are. They may not show it today, tomorrow, or the week after, but one day, for sure, they'll acknowledge you and be brought up to speed.

You'll then realize they were paying attention all along. It's so beautiful to build rapport with them and get to know each one on an individual level.

The consistency is what works for them, the routine of doing the same things over and over.

It provides a sense of stability, order, and comfort to help them understand their environment.

The List-Maker

This young lady was very smart and quick-witted. She picked up on things easily and used them to her advantage.

Brief introduction: This vivacious young lady was friendly from the start. She was playful and a bit sly but not in a bad way. She had many skills and was very advanced in her class and would complete her tasks independently and in a timely fashion–at least when she was not busy running her list of rituals. She navigated her communication device very smoothly to communicate her needs. She could type information in her device very fast and used it to express humor as well.

She was eager, energetic, and couldn't keep still, always trying to get me to do things for her and doing things she knew she shouldn't do.

She would take my hands to quickly run off her list of rituals. The list included all her daily activities from morning to evening and more.

However, it was also best not to indulge in her rituals as she would never stop.

I wouldn't oblige, but she would persist and give a smile. When she realized that I would not comply, then she would bid me farewell.

She was a smart cookie, I loved spending time with her!

There were times when she knew staff members were not looking, and she would sneak and run over to me, take my hands, and go through her list.

When she realized the staff was coming, she would smile and wave goodbye to me.

She was so precious. That was our encounter every time I visited the classroom.

She'd run over to me, shake my hands incessantly, and then try to touch whatever I was wearing that caught her eyes at that moment such as my necklaces, rings, and scarves.

She often escaped from the classroom staff when walking in the hallway near my office, and the ritual ensued.

It never failed. Occasionally, she would even sneak a hug.

It always amazes me how they would get excited and repeat the same pattern and be content with it.

The same routine was original every time in their perception. It was special for them and for me, as well.

Even though she knew that I would not partake in her list of rituals, she always tried anyway. So cute and adorable!

Building Trust

My next adorable student was a young lady who was headstrong and stubborn, a tautology that matched her perfectly. She wanted to reach out to others, but she wanted to do it in her own special way and following her own inner script.

Brief introduction: I remembered when this young lady came for a screening, which was a preadmission to the program she was not happy at all. She didn't want to be there. She was very resistance and rightly so. Being thrust into this strange place with those strange people, people that she did not know, must have been terrifying. She needed to build trust to feel safe, but that would not come easy as she was headstrong and would not let anyone draw closer to her.

Nonetheless, it remains true that it took her awhile to become acclimated in our program. I would visit her in the classroom, as often as I could. I would never stay too long, or get too close, as I knew she didn't want that. But even still, I was determined to get to know her.

Thus, when I visited, I would talk to her and offer her praise for sitting nicely; I would ask for a hi-five. At times, she would just look at me and there were times she would raise her hand to comply. It was all good.

This determined young lady would not budge when she said no to something. She was not easy to please and also had strong will.

Most of the time, she was the one in control, unfortunately, and the staff had to wait it out. Even after being in the program for years, she was resolved to seize some measure of control. Building trust and a relationship did not come easy for her.

It usually took her a while to get out of her anguish, but the staff was always patient and nurturing. As a result, at times she gave in but never totally. She was a smart young lady and she knew she was in control. Nevertheless, she was sweet in her own unique way.

She bestowed her affections upon very few, and it took her time to build rapport with others. To win her favor was a blessed thing.

It was my fortune that she took a liking to me. At times, I would use that to encourage her to comply with what she had to do, such as eating or transitioning from one place to the next.

While it was a challenge for staff to get her from one place to another, whenever I went to where she was sitting in the cafeteria or at any given location, she would extend her arm to me and would not put it down until I came to her. I would then accompany her to her destination.

That was her routine. It was her way of taking control.

When she was happy, which did not happen often, everyone was delighted because it was a rare sight.

I am happy that I was able to contribute a small part to her comfort and progress.

At times, it was best that I didn't indulge her, though it was not easy. She was always all ears when her name was being mentioned or her behavior was being discussed.

She would not be pleased, and you would know it.

I remember I had been away on vacation during the year, and on my return, I was met with a surprise.

When she laid eyes on me in the hallway, she rushed toward me with her unsteady gait to hug me and pet my cheek as if to see if I was real and give me a peck.

The staff member who was with her was astonished since she hardly ever showed affection.

It melted my heart.

It brings me joy to know that my presence had some meaning to not just her, but to all the children I interacted with and brought a smile to their faces.

It took a while to build a relationship with her and for her to come to trust me when she favored very few,

I was appreciative and delighted that she came to acknowledge me as someone who cared for her and who she liked having around.

A Gentle Soul

Once upon a time, I had the great pleasure of working with an amiable, pleasant young man who was both smart, and a gentleman.

Brief introduction: This young man never caused even a scintilla of trouble: he always faithfully complied and did what he had to do. He was friendly and one of the smartest in his class. He would often be found reading the newspaper and answering comprehensive questions.

He had a gentle soul.

Our routine was that when I visited, he would engage me in conversation about his home school district, his home address, and his mom. He would always approach me when he would see me, whether it was in or outside of his classroom.

He always wanted to talk.

He talked about visiting my office at a specific time and would call me by my full name.

He had a wonderful memory with reciting and writing his home address, district address, and school phone numbers as well as the extensions.

He was also good at math and loved to add numbers with four digits.

A visit to my office would consist of me sitting at my computer and him instructing me on what to type: his home school district, his home address, the year of his graduation, and his return home to his mom, calling her by name.

I would type out the information, and then it would be time for him to leave.

He was always a gentleman and was eager to please by attending and complying to whatever tasks he was asked to do.

Whenever and wherever he saw me, he would welcome the opportunity to repeat these rituals.

And he would wait for me to confirm that he was graduating, and that the information shared was correct.

He always looked for assurance from me regarding this information. That was our visit, and those nuances were for me and him only.

I looked forward to those special moments as they brought me much joy and inspired me.

He had to leave the school earlier than graduation, but he remembered the school number and my extension and left a few messages at night.

He was not partial to the time of day, nor did he know how to properly leave a message. It brought me to tears and melted my heart.

He was a jewel*; a gem of a jewel.*

His action was genuine and came from the heart.

Their habits, nuances, and predilections are their marks. They are who they are and should be appreciated and nurtured wholly for who they are. To be with them is to know that autism is not an insurmountable barrier to a life well-lived.

The Affectionate Heart

This next little child was so innocent, adorable, and spoke little. He mimicked often, usually remembering phrases that were taught to him and repeating them when asked.

Brief introduction: When this loveable young boy joined our program, we all were delighted. He showed affection to everyone. He was adorable. He was not interested in performing any tasks, but he was affectionate to all.

He was such a loveable young boy—a happy, cheerful, chubby, and vulnerable little fellow. This made it easy to care for him, no fuss.

He was a fresh breeze!

He loved to eat, but he didn't eat everything, or take what was not his to take. He made no demands. The staff was drawn to him. He got along with everyone and was always a joy to have around.

He would usually come to my office, sit down, and admire the photo of my daughter I had on my desk. As he looked at the picture, I would inquire who was assisting him.

Then I would see the staff follow with a smile, and they would say, "He loves you, Ingrid, and apparently your daughter, as well."

When he saw me in the hallway, he would creep up and take my hand quietly and walk with me.

I would guide him to his group, then wave goodbye. He would say, "Bye, Ingrid."

His genuine spirit just warmed my heart. He had such a beautiful soul, pure to the core.

I lived for those countless admirable and special moments with the children who had–and still have – so much to give. None of them was ever exactly the same, and each of them had something to offer that was-is priceless.

I wouldn't exchange them for anything.

The Big Whirling Dervish

I have an inexpugnable memory of one student. In my memory, this tall young man was a gentle soul who was not aware of the vital energy he emanates, or the strength that was his.

A brief background note: When I first met this tall young man, he was already in the program. I went to visit his classroom, and when I did so, he stood and walked toward me and stared at my feet. I learned later that he was staring at my high heel shoes.

He was a giant with a kind soul. Whenever I engaged with him, I literally had to raise my head up high to talk to him. He was filled with kinetic fervor and could be an inadvertent hazard. My interactions with him were marked by spinning, dancing, and being swept up in a cyclone of his own making.

He was a big whirling dervish.

I remember one day he was a bit unhappy, and he ran into me, dropping me to the floor in an instant.

He was not being aggressive toward me directly; he was running, and I happened to be in his way, and I got dropped to the floor.

Sometimes, the autistic population doesn't always acknowledge someone's presence and that's part of their characteristics. He ran into me not even acknowledging that I was there.

He was not the type to be aggressive toward others. He released tension by skipping around and he was tall. Thus, you could imagine.

His ritual, or his irrepressible expression of affection, was that he would twirl me around every time he saw me because he admired my high heel shoes. As he twirled me, he would look obsessively at my shoes. They were magnetic to him, and drew his eyes constantly.

Every time I visited his classroom, I needed to be ready on my feet, and he would have a big smile on his face as he twirled me around.

He never grew tired of twirling me around. I might have grown tired of it, from time to time, but he never did.

There were times that he would attempt to twirl me, and I would hold on to his hands and try to engage him in conversation to otherwise distract him.

It would work for a while, but then he would go back to the twirling

The teacher and classroom staff would attempt to distract him as well but to no avail.

That was our relationship. The twirling was our thing, something he did for me and for me alone, and I enjoyed it while it lasted.

I am so blessed to have been a part of their lives and journey.

The Ritualist

I was again bedazzled by another young man. He was fierce, this young one. More than you would ever know. But, at the same time, he had his favorite people, and he could be very sweet. He needed love and support but didn't always know how to go about gaining these things.

Brief history: This young man had a lot of challenge none of which he could control on his own. He was young, but very strong. And he could certainly be unpredictable: The teacher and classroom staff were always prepared for a mishap as things could change at any given time.

Every time we met, there was this hand ritual in which he would engage me. I must say that, on occasion, I would play along with some hesitation because I knew he could be unpredictable. But I needn't have worried: I didn't need to be protected from him, because all he exuded when he engaged me in this ritual was happiness and calm.

He was happy to connect with me, and I was happy he felt he could do this with me. It melted my heart.

The everyday ritual – high five, low five, fist bump, and a touch of the palm–was done slowly, but surely. And it was always done with love and assurance.

I could not have rushed it even if I wanted to, and I just had to let it run its course.

At times, the teacher would attempt to intervene or shorten the ritual. It would work sometimes, but not always.

I might have been engaged in conversation with someone and if he saw me, he would want me to stop in order to engage in his much-needed fist bump or high-five.

Yes, there were times that it was inconvenient, but nevertheless, I always welcomed it. It added something to my day, not just his, that precious little else could.

These moments were invigorating to them, something they looked forward to that somehow filled a void or provided some form of happiness.

My days were filled with heart-warming rituals that kept me going and provided me with lasting energy.

A Family of another Sort

I believe this young lady was in a bit of a quandary; she saw her parents in me. From the moment she set foot in our building, she associated me with someone familiar, someone who was important in her life. She saw me as someone who could bring her back home.

A background note: When this lovely young lady came for a screening in our program with her mother along with her twin sister, she appeared loss. She was in an environment that she didn't recognize, she needed reassurance. She didn't want to be separated from her mother. With hesitancy, she went along with me to the screening triage room where she met with our multidisciplinary team.

When I first visited with her in her classroom, the initial few days after admission into the program, she brought me to her residence as the program was a twenty-four-hour residential school.

She took my hand and led me to her bedroom, which was located on the second floor.

The school staff and I let it run its course as we wanted to understand what she was trying to non-verbally communicate.

Upon arriving in her room, she seized hold of her suitcases and readied to exit the building. I communicated to her that this was her new home using visuals.

In the school, we used Picture Exchange Communication System, also as known as PECS.

The staff member intervened after a while and brought her back down to the classroom.

I found it very interesting. She didn't choose a classroom staff or a residence staff; instead, she waited until I came to visit in the classroom.

And since then, whenever I visited her classroom, she would interact with me as if I were someone she had known in the past. She would take my hand and run it across her hair, or she would use my fingernails to provide her with hand pressure and would look at me with familiarity.

It was poignant and powerful.

This ritual went on and never stopped but after months, she finally realized that our school was her new home, and our staff was – and the other students were – her new, extended, family.

It's a funny thing, really: I have met her mother and aunt I didn't see any resemblance between myself and them. But something about me made this young lady want to connect with me and to bring me into her life.

Those special moments were only meant for me and were only shared with me.

And for that, I am in awe.

The Cheerful Angel

This young angel was **always in a cheerful mood** when I visited.

Brief introduction: This angel came to us adorable but very challenged. She was vulnerable, had no awareness of danger but was always upbeat. At times she would get too excited. I love spending time with her, though she was not one to sit still or stay in one place. She acknowledged my presence every time I visited.

She couldn't talk, but she would still come to greet me half way in the classroom, shaking her head left to right and giggling.

She would utter some sounds to share something with me, then make a sound as though she was in pain by touching her stomach.

I would sympathize and say, "you're okay," which would then make her happy. She just wanted me to acknowledge her feeling.

I looked forward to our interaction every time I visited. During my visit we would take short walks within the classroom sometime. I would compliment her on her beautiful hair and her nice outfits.

That was our little ritual, our little thing when we met with one another.

Her enthusiastic greetings always brought joy to my heart.

Seeing her happy and chuckling all the time somehow made me feel like the world was kinder, that she was in a good place.

I accepted and welcomed all of the children as they are for,

they accepted and loved me as I am with all of my weaknesses and imperfections.

Shouting from the Hilltops

As I write, all of the memories are flushing out of me.

I can picture all of my angels and their idiosyncrasies, each and every single one of them.

All of these different ballads are narrated on their own for, they are true to each of my beloved little angels

Their unique rituals and behaviors are their own and belong to only them. We are guests in their lives, and they give us joy so that we may, in turn, return that joy.

I may be narrating this story, *but it is taking place through inspiration.*

Their love and enduring humanity speak through me and come to life as written words.

Their uniqueness Must be shared,

Must be told,

Must be echoed,

And Must Be Spread.

*The world must know how loveable and precious they are, and how much joy they brought me **since they can't possibly know this themselves.***

Reading Aloud

I met this young lady in the early years of my career at our school.

Brief introduction: Her sense of humor was unique and she was so loud but didn't know it. When she was in a room everyone would notice because she would identify everything she sees and greet everyone that she knows. She never smiled and if you asked her to smile, she would show her teeth. She was too cute.

She loved to read out loud and was determined to know every word. She took her studies seriously and was always eager to learn.

She carried a book with her everywhere.

When I visited her classroom, she would stop reading, look at my badge, and greet me by my full name:

"Ingrid Jeannis-Desire, sit with me, read to me."

She would stare at me while I read. After I was done, I would tell her I had to leave.

She would then say, "Okay, Ingrid Jeannis-Desire. See you later, Ingrid Jeannis-Desire."

If any student or staff couldn't remember my full name, this student would surely remind them!

If she spotted me in the hallway, she would come to a stop and greet me by my full name, then depart with,

"See you later, Ingrid Jeannis-Desire."

Somehow, as soon as she said it, the day became brighter and better.

A Bubbly Personality

Oh, my! I feel very sentimental as I reminisce about this young man who was so full of life.

A brief note: He came to us on the first day with his bubbly and vivacious self. He kept interrupting us as we were talking. He was friendly, funny, and talked incessantly. We couldn't stop him even if we tried.

When you were around him, you just couldn't help but love him or laugh with him.

He would carry a conversation while laughing and crying at the same time. Then he would become serious, as if the laughter had to be balanced out by a more pensive side that intermittently revealed itself.

He was bubbly with a high pitch voice. You could not mistake his voice: he was unique and funny and loving.

When he was not having a good day, the entire classroom could feel it because the bubbliness was no longer there.

The classroom would turn quiet—no noise, no complaint, no calling out, no jokes.

Yet if he heard that I was on the way or if he heard my voice, he would start calling out for me to come.

When I approached him, he was very happy! He would then complain to me about being sick or hungry.

Out of the blue, he would take my hand to attempt to dance without any coordination.

We had fun together. I couldn't be any happier when I was around him as he was so funny. I don't think he knew that.

He had a such a good heart!

I would spot him in the parking lot on my way home after work, and he would start calling out my name while he approached me.

I often needed to remind him to wait for staff and not take off without supervision, but he would say with a sad face,

"But, Ingrid, I wanted to see you and say hi…"

It was all love! I was blessed to have had the company of this young man and all of those angels around me.

Their idiosyncrasies, and their expressions of love, melt my heart away

This journey of my life is unforgettable and all worthwhile.

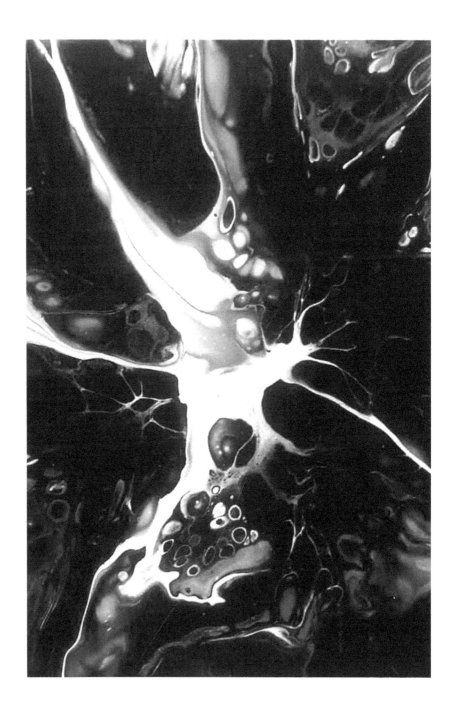

Shutters to a Beautiful Soul

My next beautiful student was a medium-sized, but touchingly tender, young man. There was never a need to worry about him – not about anything.

His background: He came to us quiet and shy; never expressed any anger and he showed very little interest in participating in activities. He needed encouragement to get involved in activities. His personality never wavered even after being in the program for years.

He didn't ask for anything and was content to just be.

If you didn't address him, you wouldn't know he had needs.

When I visited the classroom, I would stop by his desk, converse with him, and give him some attention. Goodness knows, he never asked for any attention for himself

He would sit quietly at his desk and would not initiate anything unless the teacher and classroom staff engage him.

When I spoke to him, he would close his eyes and reopen them, then close them again as if he was playing hide and seek.

One day, one of the staff said, "Wait a minute!

He only behaves like that when he sees Ingrid. Ingrid, I think he enjoys seeing you!"

He would then look a little, then close his eyes again.

That became our little moment.

He would see me, then close his eyes, but not fully.

I would engage him in conversation, then as I was leaving, he would open his eyes once more.

How could I ever forget these tender moments?

They are the children themselves.

It is who they are. Precious!

His eyelids were shutters that, when opened, revealed a beautiful soul.

The Silent Hand-Holder

My next story is about still another wonderful young person who made my life better by being a part of it. He was a quiet little boy who couldn't talk and didn't do much.

Some background: This little boy was an enigma for us: very challenged, nonverbal. There was not much to go on with given the fact that family involvement was minimal to nonexistence. Our staff took special care of him and made him feel at home.

Sometimes, the staff and I wondered if he was aware of anything that was happening around him.

But after several contacts with him, he began to always stand up and hold on to my hand when I would approach his desk and call out his name.

I would talk to him, ask how he was doing even though I knew I wouldn't receive a reply.

He would just hold on to my hands while turning his head clockwise.

I'm not sure if he'd ever look into my eyes.

Nevertheless, he knew it was me, and he acknowledged that I was there to spend time with him.

It was our thing, our little ritual, and forging that connection with him was like building one part of a larger foundation that I dare say that we gave to each other.

I appreciated those moments with him and I looked forward to reconnecting each and every time I visited him.

"Pitsa"

My next little jewel didn't ask much, but was as happy as could be.

Little background: I remembered when she first arrived in our school, very tenacious. It was hard to find reinforcers to help her, but the teacher and staff members were persistent and eventually, they won her over. Eureka, we found the one thing that would change her behavior and encourage her to complete short tasks: the iPad! Slowly but surely, she came to understand and make connection with having the iPad to compliant and demonstrate appropriate behavior. It was a win-win.

Our relationship grew along the way. Every time I visited, she would run to me, bounce up and down, and echo the same word "Pitsa" with a big smile on her face.

I would try to get some words in, but she wouldn't pay any attention.

She would just smile, bounce up and down, and repeat, "Pitsa."

When I tried to leave, she held onto my hands tightly and smiled.

She was content with that, and I was content with her.

I looked forward to seeing her smile and to seeing her feel happiness. Her joy brought me joy. The sunshine in her eyes was the sunshine that lit up my day.

Our exchanges were often brief, but they were always enough to bring a smile to my face.

Short but sweet.

The Steel-Trap Mind

Each of these children has a talent, some more visible than others.

The young lady about whom I am thinking now was a young lady with great talent. She remembered, it seemed, everything, and her memories were always vivid and evocative. Her brilliance drew you in like a steel trap.

Brief introduction: This lovely young lady challenged us so many times. It was not easy to win her over. It was an in-progress type of situation. Never knew what would hit you or how it would hit you; just had to be always prepared. And still, we didn't always get it right. And that was okay for it was what it was. The learning curve was continuous, there was no end date as their behaviors changed all the time for whatever reasons. We just needed to be on our games always. Staff were amazing!

One would only have to mention a certain year, and she would recount in an orderly fashion all the major events that transpired in that particular year. And she would so with no hesitancy or doubt.

Even once a birth date was shared with her, she would retain it forever, and would be quick to inform one of all the eventful undertakings that took place in that special year.

She always looked forward to sharing my personal information with me and I would enthusiastically thank her for it.

I had never encountered one so blessed as to be able to remember so many things that, on their surface, were not at all easy to recall. What a unique gift! What a unique blessing!

The skills and talents of these children are quite unique and distinctive, *owned only by them, and in service only to God.*

The Conversationalist

This young man came to us at a later age than most of our children. He was smart, observant, and spoke fast. He always had things to say.

Brief introduction: When he first arrived, he was very anxious, pacing back and forth and feeling loss. I believed it was a shock to him coming to this new place and not knowing any one or what to expect. But soon, he settled in and became comfortable and befriended some of the staff.

He used to call me "Ms. Ingrid."

He would ask why some of his classmates couldn't talk or why they were doing other things.

When he thought I was not paying attention, he would say,

"Ms. Ingrid, Ms. Ingrid!"

I would call out his name and reply, "Yes, I'm listening."

Then he would continue his story.

I would encourage him to complete his tasks, especially math as he loved mathematics and was good at it.

Our visits would always entail him recounting events that are not relatable and I would engage him in conversation that required him to focus on the present.

He would reply most of the time as he understood what I was saying.

But when he didn't want to comply… oh, boy!

He would do a merry-go-round with me!

Here is a good example. One day, he had gone on his weekly shopping trip with his class.

Normally, he would be excited to share with me what he and his classmates had done on the trip and what he had purchased.

That day, he was in a mood and not having any of it.

I asked him, "Where did you go?"

He replied, "Somewhere."

I asked, "What did you buy?"

He replied, "Something."

I asked, "What is that something?"

He said, "Don't know."

I asked, "Who did you go with?"

He said, "No one."

When he saw me the next day, without me asking him anything, he volunteered the information that I had asked him about the day *before.*

He said, "Ms. Ingrid, Ms. Ingrid, I apologize! I went to the supermarket With Ms. _____ and my friends, and I purchased a soda."

I thanked him for sharing with me and smiled.

He knew what he was doing and remembered that he hadn't told me the truth.

That was our little thing, our ritual. He was testing me, but in a joyous and loving manner. And each time that we interacted, that bond between us wound a little bit tighter. AND I FOUND GREAT ENJOYMENT IN EACH ONE.

TIS who they are, loving fun, and all that comes with them.

I loved speaking to him and getting him to engage in conversation.

Every Day Is a "Goood" Day

This young man was special and very unpredictable for we never knew what to expect, though our staff prepared for every possible contingency.

Background: This special young man was a force to be reckoned with, subtle but sharp. He was not easy to engage but once you knew what he needed and when to intervene, you had won a gold medal. He didn't take too much into any one or anything. The key was building the right relationship with him and putting in place the right behavior plan that would set him up for success.

He did not independently initiate conversation, did not speak much, and did not require much as long as his behavior plan was being followed accordingly. However, he would initiate and attend to his basic needs.

I reckon he understood much more than he led on.

He was a force, but the sweetest young man ever. He had a very special relationship with one of the classroom staff.

You only needed to know how to interact with him and anticipate his needs.

Our relationship was built on trust and understanding. When I visited his classroom, I would approach his desk where he oftentimes would have his head down or covered with a sheet. Our interactions often seemed to start the same way.

I would say, "Hi, _____."

He would uncover his head, look up, give me a toothy smile, and say "Goood."

I would extend my hand for a low five, and he would give me one.

I would ask to see his work, and he would show it to me. I'd praise him, and he would, again, give me a toothy smile.

I always looked forward to seeing his beautiful smile and hearing him say, "Goood," before I could even ask how he was. As long as I knew he was safe and protected, every day was a "Goood" day.

That was our way of building a link between us that would endure the rough times as well as the better ones, and it was very special to me.

Each one of these children has something unique and personal to offer

We only need to get to know them to appreciate all their attributes.

From the Heart

Kindness comes in small packages and oftentimes doesn't require much effort because it comes from the heart. It is that pure love that is given naturally.

Our children don't ask for much. They are *not asking for expensive gifts.*

They just want some kindness; the simplest kind of gesture—*a kind word, a gentle touch, a warm expression, a loving smile, a form of guidance,* **or a nurturing hand; these are often the only things they need from us.**

Pure and simple. **Nothing complicated.**

We often think an act of kindness requires a lot, but it is such a simple thing to be kind, and it rarely costs one anything. And to be kind to children who need it is the noblest and most selfless thing one can do. It will gratify you as nothing else will.

It is beautiful because **it comes from the heart.**

By practicing kindness, you add years onto your life.

It is a win-win!

It softens your heart and helps you focus to what's important; the interaction with each other.

A simple act of kindness can provoke such powerful emotion.

So, when you think of the children, think of kindness.

A Firm Grasp and a Sweet Soul

My handsome little fellow was a sweet hyper-active child who was always out of breath.

He liked to touch things and put them in his mouth.

Some background: He came to our program, running all over and had to be chased. Parents were not able to sustain him thus, our multidisciplinary team had to intervene to settle him down. It was not easy. He was grabbing and pinching and rightly so, this environment and the people were new to him. Always keep in mind that adjusting to new environment or new things is not the strength of an autistic person, they struggle to novelty. They are use with routines and schedules, doing same things over and over thus, providing them with a sense of stability and safety. Even then, these routines can be a challenge at times, as they are constantly evolving.

He was very unaware of things around him and had no sense of danger or of the things that were inedible. He ingested anything.

Thus, *close* supervision was necessary.

He couldn't talk and would not always interact with others.

However, over the course of several weeks, we built a friendship. Whenever I visited, **he would hold on to my hands and squeeze them for a while.**

He would then pace back and forth while he squeezed my hand. Nothing to be alarmed about: he just needed the reassurance of knowing that my hand was there, just as I was there, to give him support should he need it.

It may seem a trifle, but such daily rituals gave me an almost inexpressible joy, and he never failed to repeat them whenever I was present: whether in the classroom or art class or gym class or music class, the ritual touched us both and made me appreciate how much I had made the right choice to become a part of this wonderful world filled with wonderful children.

That was our routine, and I relished it every time.

These children's love was so genuine and innocent.

It's priceless.

Our children are open vessels, ready to be taught, led, inspired, and transformed.

Laughter through a Lifetime

There are certain things that can't be bought, and laughter is one of them.

To share laughter is to give a gift, and, boy, those children brought so much laughter every day! A healthy laughter, the kind of laughter that enriches a life and adds something to it that is hard to capture in words.

Laughter is also a blessing, and blessings also can't be bought.

I cherished those children and all that they were and are, ***idiosyncrasies-quirks and all.***

The memories are all that I have left to embrace, **and every time I reminisce about them,** they bring me laughter and joy, and they warm my heart with happy remembrances.

The Sharp Dresser

*My next friend was a dashing young man **who took pride in the way he dressed** and in his wide selections of ties.*

Some background: This young dasher was an orphan when he arrived in our program. He was a polite and friendly young boy who grew up into a dashing young man in our program. As with all the students, his needs needed to be attended to and managed, but it was not a problem as he was one of the calmest among the students. He wanted to be perceived as a grown up; thus, he was always striking a conversation with adults.

When I visited the classroom, he would approach me to make sure that I noticed his outfit.

I would compliment him, of course, and he would say with great enthusiasm, "Thank you, Ms. Ingrid!"

He was aware of hierarchy structures and knew that the Principal of the school had all the power.

Thus, he would ask me to order more books for the library or tell me That I was a good principal and then shake my hand.

He would ask about what I did in my office, and I'd share a few things.

He would then say, "Thank you, Ms. Ingrid the Principal. I'll see you tomorrow," and shake my hand.

I would then reply, "I'll see you tomorrow..."

That was our little ritual each time we met, and I loved it and treasured it. *You could see him striving to make a positive difference in the world, and I loved him for it.*

We marvel at them as they marvel at us.

Blowing Kisses

This young lady was as special as they come.

She was silly and strong-willed, *yet loveable.* **She was a social butterfly who loved to greet everyone and blow kisses.**

Little history about her: She was an impetuous, adorable young lady who was always getting into mischief. With her strong will, it was always hard to get her to complete an entire task and focus when she only wanted to do her own thing. It was not that she was not capable of doing the task; in fact, she was quite smart. If you interrupted her scripts she would be upset and might even strike but nothing major to worry about: she was not one to remain upset for long.

She was a busy body and when transitioning to a new location, she would stop in every corner to count and touch everything within her path.

When I visited the classroom, I would stop by her desk and gave her one-on-one attention to encourage her to do task. At times, with some luck, she would join me and do some work.

We developed a relationship along the way during my many visits in the classroom and other settings. I took an interest in her and she in turn began to look forward to seeing me and interacting with me daily.

During my visits, she would call upon me to come to her. She loved to kiss and would kiss my hand, but I would redirect her to shake my hand instead.

She would ask me in her eccentric, shaky but sweet voice, "Ingrid, sit with me," and point to a chair.

She would then proceed to count by touching invisible things on her desk and say, "Ingrid, stay with me," *while holding my hand.*

I would stay with her for a while. When it was time for me to leave, she would attempt to kiss my hand again **and say, "Bye bye, Ingrid," and blow me kisses.**

That was our little thing, and our time spent together was always special.

Our children are of pure heart, they give selflessly and unconditionally, like the God who created us.

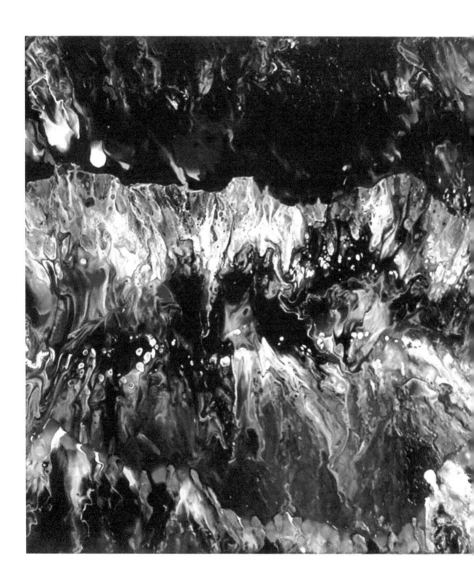

To Love or Not to Love?

My relationship with this young lady was one of love, but with tension occasionally surfacing.

A little history about our lovely young lady: She wreaked havoc as her symptoms were severe. She was anguished often. Special accommodation within the classroom was needed for her for example, making her space entirely separate from the rest of the students, providing certain protective measures to ensure safety for both she and her classmates- and staff as well. She was struggling with her illness a lot, but it did not prevent her from showing affection when she was in a good place. Our children showed grace even in the darkest times.

I built a rather seemingly relationship with her from a far. At times, she would seek out my company. Other times, she would not need my presence.

Either way, she would make it known to me.

If she was feeling happy, *I would come in the classroom, and she would call out my name repeatedly.*

She would share her work with me, and I would praise it.

She would willingly read to me and give me one of her completed tasks as a gift.

However, when her mood was different, the moment she heard my voice, she would call out,

"No, Ingrid! *No, Ingrid! Go, go!"*

I never took it personally for I knew this was part of who they were.

I just waited patiently, knowing that when the time was right, *she would be ready to welcome me, and I would be ready to receive her with open arms!*

Then we were back to being good friends and the cycle would continue.

That was our relationship, **and I embraced it all!**

Evidently, my presence meant something to her, and I appreciated her just the way she was—

An imperfect, loveable human being.

The Smart, Silent Type

This young man was smart and very shy. He knew how to write, read, and could work independently. But he had a defiant streak, and many was the time when he would keep his talents hidden from us, or simply refuse to use them.

Some History: This young man had many skills and chose not to put them to practice. The fault was not entirely his as he was never taught to challenge himself prior to coming to our program. He lived at home with his parents who did not speak English. When letters were sent home, he would decide which letters he would share with his parents. Smart young man, wasn't he? We knew he could do so much. He needed many positive reinforcers to share his skills with us. It was not an easy task.

Many times, he would refuse to do any work. It was sometimes his way of testing us. Other times, he was just plain not interested in doing any work. But classroom staff was always determined to win him over.

It took some effort to get him to engage, but when he did, the staff and I were amazed and proud at the same time! He knew what to do and did it well in the nick of time.

By then, we formed a bond. Whenever I visited his classroom, he would give me a shy smile.

The teacher would ask, "Are you shy because INGRID is here? Why don't you show Ingrid what you can do?"

He would look at me, look down at his work, and then look elsewhere.

Our moments of bonding happened every time I came in the classroom. When I approached his desk, he would smile shyly and never talk, though he knew how to.

I would praise him on whatever task he was working on.

He would look at me, tilt his head to the side, and smile, then look elsewhere.

This happened the entire time I was in his company.

As I left and waved goodbye, he would look at me again and smile.

That was our time together.

Whatever the children had to offer was welcomed. If redirection was needed, then I would apply it.

Their interactions with me – and with others – were marked by so much that was natural, delightful, loveable, harmless, innocent.

And, above all else, achingly sincere. They brought much joy to me.

Miracles Every Day

We often don't realize it or see it, but miracles are happening in our lives daily.

Perhaps we don't notice them because we are expecting something of great magnitude, something awesome or even inexplicable. Perhaps we seek something far beyond the ordinary, not appreciating that it is the little mercies and blessings that make up a good life. But I can assure you that the little things count for almost everything.

Their immense value is there in the joy we receive from one another...

The laughter that fills our heart...

The warmth that brings us comfort...

The love that shines and transforms our soul...

The social interaction that keeps us going...

Those happy times are the golden threads that are interwoven and make us whole. They are the threads that weave together a live.

The seemingly small, blessed moments are the miracles of life. The daily things that make us smile or connect us with others are the treasures that we inherit but to which we are often blind.

It is our human tendency to focus on the struggle, to believe that our lives were not meant to be easy, that we were not meant to be happy or fortunate.

The imperfection seems to be closer to home, feels to fit in better than the pure love, joy, and laughter that was destined for us.

Some people grow up and spread cheer while others don't.

Our autistic children, despite their struggles and the often insurmountable obstacles they face, spread cheer and create miracles, not even aware of the impact they have on the lives of those around them.

Could you imagine that the most precious thing in life is actually free of charge?

It is given freely and wholeheartedly, with no hassle, by ordinary human beings.

The children taught us that life is not that serious.

We should all live as though someone is writing a book about us.

Making a Connection

This little lovely boy did not know how to show others that he needed attention and affection.

Brief introduction: When this little boy came to our school, he appeared lost. He was very energetic and did not know how to interact properly without causing injury. But, in time, with a customized behavior management plan, he learned how to communicate better.

When I visited the classroom, he would quickly leave his chair, *come to me, pull my hand, pinch me,* and then give me an innocent smile.

Thus, I knew he was not acting with malice. He just didn't know how to communicate.

Once I realized what was happening, I became proactive and would attempt to hold on to his hands while we interacted.

Every time I visited, I went by his desk, gently took his hand, and held onto it while I talked to him.

He would smile at me, so I knew he enjoyed my company because he would always get excited when he saw me.

I wanted the experience to be joyful, and wanted *him to know how to interact with others properly,*

The appropriate behavior was being reinforced in the classroom.

Eventually, he learned, and when he saw me, He would quickly run to me, **stop in front of me, and smile.**

This became our little routine.

Afterwards, I would take his hands and walk back with him to his desk and spend some time with him or even read a short book to him.

Then I would wave goodbye, and he would smile and wave.

I looked forward to our visits, and I appreciated it a great deal every time I visited with him.

Communicating without Words

My next story revolves around a special young lady who was nonverbal.

Brief history: She came in our program, very quiet, smiling and blinking her eyes. When we spoke to her, she would blink her eyes and uttered some sounds very fast. The parents were from a foreign land thus, at times, we thought she was communicating through that language in her own way. But we never knew.

I always took a special interest to our new admits specifically and set times aside to get to know to them.

Every time I came to the classroom, she would come and greet me, blink her eyes, and uttered something fast and not quite clear if she was speaking a different language

She would take my hands and bring me to her desk all the while echoing what sounded to be foreign words and give me a smile.

I was not aware of if she knew what she was saying. I did ask her dad if she spoke or understood their language.

Her father told me that they spoke it to her at home but were not sure if she understood. It would appear she did process and retain some part of the language. This is just speculation.

And, each time it was time for us to part, I would say goodbye to her, and she would be all ready for me to go.

She would walk me to the door and slam it behind me

Every time I think of this scenario, I can't help but laugh out loud.

I understood their gist, and I loved them, which is why I call them the little quirks that melt my heart.

As I said, I don't think she knew what she was saying to me, but she attempted to communicate with me in her own way and interacted with me the only way she knew how.

I cherished that!

All the children were my precious gems. They opened their heart to us and said,

"This is me.

Accept me as I am."

Eternally Grateful

I am grateful for whatever those children saw in me that gave them comfort and made them happy whenever we interacted.

I was and still feel so honored and consider all of these interactions as blessings.

In all of my imagination, I never expected to be wrapped up with so much affection for these children.

Love is the most powerful agent of change. It shines and evokes change naturally.

Our children don't have eyes for faults.

They can only see virtues and goodness in all.

It's only fair that we see them for the angels that they are.

And give them back the unconditional love they bequeath to us.

The Little Things Are the Big Things

The little things in retrospect are often the things that turned out to be the most meaningful— the little things are the big things in life, even if you might never notice until it is almost too late

The smallest things in life *are often the most precious.*

Take babies, for example. They are so small, yet infinitely treasured, so vital in all our lives.

The saying that good things come in small packages has often proven true.

*Our autistic children may have limitations, as we all have limitations**, but they are enormous in their kindness and love!***

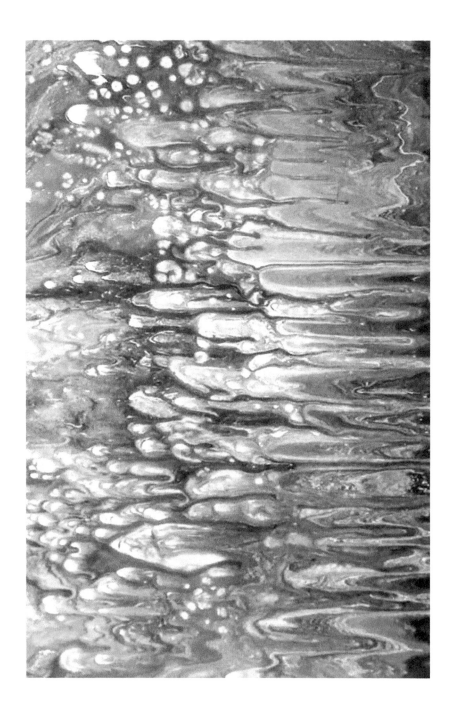

Conclusion

Our autistic population is a population filled with innocents who earnestly express how they feel, and who want only our love and respect in turn. By giving them love, we exercise our fullest human potential for goodness and for giving back to the world around us.

You only need to know them *to fall in love.*

And more than that, by building a relationship with them, you grow beyond your former boundaries and limitations. Building rapport with them is the key to this population's heart.

It is crucial that you allow yourself to get to know them and afford them the opportunity to trust you and know that they can rely upon you.

It is so important that they know how special they are in your eyes, and this manifests itself in how you care for them and treat them.

The autistic population is vulnerable in the sense that they come to us with an open heart saying,

"This is me. **This is who I am.** Please accept me."

Once you have established a relationship with them, it is a different world, a different ballgame.

You not only open up the world for you to help them, but you open up the world for them, too. *And you open up new energies and vistas within yourself, too.*

You give them hope, a fighting chance, a chance to discover themselves, for some of them don't know who they are or what they are capable of doing. And they give you a powerful reason to be the best person you can be, each and every day.

With time, you come to know what to expect and how to care for them. When this happens, everything becomes better, clearer, and manageable.

You plan for them, so that they might be safer and more secure. They feel safer because plans are put in place to protect them, to teach them, and to guide them; they also understand that there are people to whom they can turn when they feel vulnerable or even helpless.

There is no greater joy and accomplishment than when you are working to create a positive change and finally see that change in them.

When they get it, (and perhaps understand what you are doing and why you are doing it), it makes all the work and effort worthwhile!

We not only save the children, but they save us, as well.

We learn to care in a manner that we didn't think we could.

We give love in a way we didn't think we could.

At school, our autistic children became our children away from home.

We cared for them, protected them, and attended to them as though they were our very own, and we were all blessed to have had the opportunity to work with them.

If you can help someone without any expectation of reward,

You become someone magical.

All it takes is love and a little bit of kindness.

You see, most of us have the magic in us. We need to give ourselves a chance to share and create special moments for those who are in need.

Don't sell yourself short. *Almost all of us have some goodness in us, waiting to be set forth upon the world.*

Working with these children makes us better; it makes us stand taller.

It attests to our strength, to our selfless love, and to our patience and our human way.

We have had to learn again and again until we got things right.

And thanks to the children and our love for them, we stood up to the test!

We prevailed!

We made a difference in their lives, and it was beautiful!

As we watched their progress *Unfold, there was no greater joy!*

To have had the opportunity to make a difference in the lives of **one,**

    two,

        three,

            and many more unique and loving souls.

What a blessing*!* What a legacy to pass on to others.

How fortunate we were to be given the opportunity to school these children and turn their lives around.

Those changes impacted their lives

                for the better eternally.

It gave them a chance to:

- be independent,
    - make choices
- have structure in their lives,
- have other ways to do things,
    - express their needs,
- socialize without or with little fear,
    - navigate their world,
- communicate,
- be in control of their feelings,
    - know that they are loved,
- make sense of their lives,
    - have familiarity,
- have predictability,

- feel at home

o and be at home in a special place they can call home

We provided the children with the proper tools and the opportunity to interact with their families;

with the feelings of steadfastness,
happiness,
comfort,
And love.

Love changes all and we provided them with the ultimate- *LOVE

We found the love in them, and their love was reflected in us.

They made us better people just by being themselves.

The autistic population has given us the gift of life. I don't think they are aware of just—How precious they are!

How loved they are!

On their behalf,

Thank you, to those who work with them and to their parents, their friends, and their families.

The autistic population is love, iconic in their own nature, and truly a blessing.

THE SPLENDOR OF GOD

Note from the Author

Thank you for the opportunity to share my stories with all of you. They may not be epochal in scale, but they are important to me. And I think they are the kind of stories that can help all of us embrace not only our own humanity, but the humanity of those of us who are different.

It has been a joyful ride for me.

I hope you have enjoyed each and every one of them as much as I have.

From my heart to yours- my friends,

Ingrid Jeannis-Desire

About the Author

Ingrid Jeannis-Desire is a woman of great passion with a positive outlook on life who believes that life offers infinite possibilities; all each of us need to do is to find the right pathway. She presently lives in New York with her husband and daughter.

She is a retiree in the educational system, but not from learning as life is its own teacher. She is a life-long learner who relishes discovering and learning new things each day. She works on projects that promote the welfare of humanity. Life, after all, is about improvement and empowerment.

She devoted a major part of her life as a teacher, a counselor, and school administrator. Her degrees in the field of psychology, special education, guidance and school counseling, school leadership, and counseling psychology, ranging from the levels of bachelor through doctorate, has paved the path for her many accomplishments. She is grateful for all her experiences, and especially grateful at how they have helped her become the person she is today.

Her journey with the autistic population was God-sent. God knew what He was doing when He placed her in that school. This experience, this journey transformed her life forever.

Her email contact:
littlequirksthatmeltmyheart@yahoo.com

Website: withgracebook.com

Acknowledgements

To my amazing daughter Desi who inspires me as she pursues her journey of becoming a copy editor, and to my loving husband Garry for his unwavering love and support. Thank you both for all the love!

About the young artist behind the paintings on the cover and inside this book:

Alizée Saint-Louis is a talented emerging young artist who is a part of the autistic population. Her works are skillful, beautiful, and expressive. Alizée, thank you for your valuable contribution. Keep painting!

Ingram Content Group UK Ltd.
Milton Keynes UK
UKHW020202150423
420187UK00001B/10